Tender

Whispers

of the

Heart

"Poems and
Other Writings"

Violet I. Escalera

ISBN: 9798352227961

Dedication

I want to especially dedicate this book to my husband. Through the years, he has encouraged me to write poems. Even when I felt they weren't great, he continued encouraging me. He is also the one who patiently waited for me to finish writing. Each time, he urged me on and mentioned the possibility of publishing them at some point. Without him, I wouldn't have gotten this far.

Acknowledgments

There are many people I want to thank for their help or simply for their encouragement.

First, as I wrote out a journal for my grandson, I realized how many poems I had written. Both my grandson and son told me how much they liked my poems so I decided it was time to publish it. Thanks to both of you and my daughter-in-law for your encouragement!

Second, I thank my children for their patience with me. Although, not all my children had a poem written about them by me, I hope you understand. My goal is to write something for each of you. I love all of you, including the one I lost in the early years of marriage. I pray for all of you regularly!

Third, I thank my mom, Marietta, for her encouragement.

Fourth, I thank Alison Phillips for coming up with the name of the book.

Last of all, thank you to everyone in my life who encouraged me in my writing, suggested names for the book, or even listened to me tell about what I had written! I appreciate it very much. Each word of encouragement kept me going. A huge thanks to each of you!

Table of Contents

Chapter 1 Serious Poems About the Lord

Chapter 2 Light-hearted
Poems

Chapter 3 Dealing With Death…

Chapter 4 Familiar Tunes With New Words

Chapter 5 Persecution

Chapter 6 Sister
Poems

Chapter 7 Some Grandson Poems

Chapter 8 Husband Poems

Chapter 9 Miscellaneous Poems Through the Years

Chapter 10 Relationship Poems

Chapter 11 Abortion Poems

Chapter 12 All About Time

Chapter 13 Monologues and Short Stories

Chapter 1

Serious Poems

about the Lord

Remind My Heart

When the struggles come
And my heart is pained within me
When the doubts arise
And I cannot clearly see Thee
When the fears assail
And I respond so brokenly
Remind my heart that You are in control!

When the strength I had
Or once thought I had alludes me
And the shadows stretched
Before me so I cannot see
And the darkness clouds
My eyes so that I do fail Thee
Remind my heart that You are in control!

Lord, You are my light
There is none e'er to fear but Thee
You're my strength and life
When it seems that the enemy
Comes to eat my flesh
Help me not to fear but believe
Remind my heart that You are in control!

7-12-2017

I wrote this one when I looked at the circumstances instead of the Lord of the circumstances. Always remember that God is in control no matter what happens in your life!

****

None But You

Who do I have in heaven but You
I look on earth and none are true
Your Word says all men are liars
Regardless of whatever transpires
I know You will see me through
Give strength in this situation, too!

There is none on earth but You I desire
To Your Word I can go and inquire
What is right, what is wrong and do
Right with joy and delight for You
Naught of this world's goods to acquire
Because You are my only true Supplier

My flesh and heart continually fails You
It seems no matter what I try to do
What I want as my wish and desire
You have to take me through that fire
To teach my heart to be ever true
Because only You can guide me through.

You are my strength and the entire
Portion of my heart You will acquire
Forever and ever You will imbue
Me with Your Word and life that's new
So the praise with what will transpire
Me doing Your will is Yours only and entire.

6-20-2017

Two of my favorite verses are Psalm 73:25-26. Because of this, I felt impressed to write up a poem about how God is my desire, my portion. No matter how much your heart fails, if you make God your portion forever, you will have delight in His presence.

****

When Sadness…

When sadness wells up within the soul
Turn, turn, turn to the Lord
Grab, grab, grab to His Word
Pray, pray, pray for His faith
When sadness wells up within the soul!

When problems and trials come your way
Ask, ask, ask for His aid
Trust, trust, trust don't forsake
Stand, stand, stand still and wait
When problems and trials come your way!

When the agony of heart prevails
Run, run, run to the One
Who only can satisfy
Hold tight until it's in the past
When the agony of heart prevails!

3-20-2016

Life isn't easy. The only way we can get through is by being in God's Word and praying. Don't wait to do this when you are going through a rough time. Is it easy right now? Then spend time in God's Word and pray. He will help you through those times that will come. Is it rough right now? He alone can give you the peace that passes all understanding. Run to His Word and pray!

****

God Is Good All the Time!

So when things look dreary and sad
When I no longer feel like I'm glad
When things are painful, I might add
God is good all the time
And all the time God is good!

When I'm struggling and life seems blue
And all the things that I'm going through
People take it and purposely construe
God is good all the time
And all the time God is good!

When the heartbreak just wears me down
In my sorrows, I feel like I'm about to drown
Most people just look at me with a frown
God is good all the time
And all the time God is good!

When the agony of life hurts my heart
and those I thought loved me depart
And from death's door comes a dart
God is good all the time
And all the time God is good!

Whatever the problem or trial ahead
Whatever might hurt you or you might dread
Whatever you go through think instead
God is good all the time
And all the time God is good!

7-10-2017

When we lived in Liberia, we often heard the phrase, "God is good all the time." This would elicit the response of others, "All the time God is good!" No matter what happens in our lives, God is always good. Praise the Lord for that fact because we can look to Him and know that He is in control and will do what is right!

****

The Lord Is...

The Lord Is...
My very strong tower and fortress
To Whom I run to
And I am safe
When it seems like all of the stress
Of life runs me through
And then I chafe
Instead of moving forward to press
On so I can do
God's plan fail safe.

The Lord Is…
The Strengthener of my life and heart
He will give me peace
To follow Him
Unless I think I am way too smart
Do His will I'll cease
Then pride does brim
May He help me to make a new start
My pride to decrease
My will to trim.

The Lord Is...
Perfect in all His ways and my Light
He helps me see truth
And do His good
Instead I listen and then invite
Darkness and uncouth
Lies, my eyes hood
Turn me back, may my heart be contrite
Let God be my sleuth,
Sin be withstood.

The Lord Is...
The One Who brings forth my righteousness
And judgment when those
Believe me wrong
It's so easy to be contentious
When I'm right...suppose
I am so strong
Lord, please help me to show graciousness
Which from You, yes, shows
You are my song.

7-28-2016

The Lord is all we need. It is always best to turn to Him for help in every situation even when it is hard.

****

Let Us Praise the Lord!

Is your day going wrong?
Your heart feeling sad?
And your life falling apart?
Let us praise the Lord!

Great is Your faithfulness,
Great is Your lovingkindness,
Great is Your mercifulness!
Let us praise the Lord!

Did someone break your heart?
Did someone disappoint you?
Did someone discourage your way?
Let us praise the Lord!

Praise Him for His mighty acts!
Praise Him for His greatness!
Praise Him for His infinite understanding!
Let us praise the Lord!

Did life let you down?
Did a friend leave you?
Did you lose someone dear to you?
Let us praise the Lord!

He heals the broken in heart!
He binds up their wounds!
He lifts up the meek!
Let us praise the Lord!

8-6-2015

I wrote this one while in the middle of one of the hardest times in my life! The truth is that we should praise the Lord no matter what happens around us because God is always worthy of praise. He controls all situations!

****

Be Still

Be still and know that I am God
How hard it is this way to trod
I seek to be still and to know
But what happens is there to show
That my mind wanders far away
And I realize I'm not still today
I grow flustered and on edge
Even though once anew I pledge
To not let it happen ever again
Wouldn't you know it then
It happens once more, yes, to me
I think it does so I will see
That I need to depend on Him
So I won't go with just any whim
I'm so thankful to His Word
He is always undeterred
He truly knows what He is doing
And soon He is accomplishing
What is needed in my heart
Since it takes trials to impart
That stillness to know He alone
Is always on His eternal throne.

7-2-2017

The day I wrote this my heart was definitely not still. I couldn't seem to focus on the Lord. Now, I realize that I didn't stay in God's Word, I didn't pray, and I definitely wasn't obedient to forgive my enemies. When we follow God, He will bring peace to our hearts and even heal them despite what others do to us. I ask that you be willing to forgive your enemies or those you think are your enemies and follow God with all of your heart.

"Jesus was born to die so that we would die to ourselves and live for Him."

12-15-2015

****

Psalm 63

My soul thirsteth for You
My flesh longeth for You
In a dry and thirsty land
where no water is.
Oh God, Thou art my God!

To see Your great power
To see Your great glory
As I have seen You in
the sanctuary
Oh God, Thou art my God!

Because Your lovingkindness
Is better than life to me
My lips shall sing praise
to Your holy name
Oh God, Thou art my God!

And bless You while I live
I lift my hands to You, Lord
My soul shall be content
with Your provisions
Oh God, Thou art my God!

When I think about You
At night upon my bed

And ponder Your Word
in the dead of night
Oh God, Thou art my God!

Because You are my help
So in Your shadow I'll sing
My soul delights in You and
Your hand strengthens me
Oh God, Thou art my God!

11-17-2021

As I learned this chapter, it's had an impact on my life. God is always there no matter what. I did try to set this to music, but couldn't seem to get the right tune. Still, I enjoyed writing it.

****

I'll Worship You In Truth and Love

My heart will sing and glorify my God
I'll worship You in truth and love
My God, my Rock, You are the One Who guides me
The One Who keeps me safely while I sleep

You are my Light, the One Whose Name is holy
The One Who does whatever He has pleased
My peace, my Lord, You are my true Redeemer
The One Who's more to be desired than gold

Who gives the truth, Who's righteous altogether
You guide my way and bring me to Your fold
My Lawgiver, One Who wrote commandments
The One Who keeps my feet from stumbling

My Confidence, the One Who sits in heaven
Who brings forth judgment when it is hidden

8-21-2021

Remember, God is all these things no matter what happens in your life. Turn to Him and be willing to wait for His mercy and judgment in everything!

****

"Man will fail you so do not depend on him for filling that empty spot in your heart. Turn to the Lord and His Word as only He can make you whole!"

12-2-2015

Chapter 2

Light-hearted

Poems

Too Tired To Think

(Not sure that I care…)
As I wake up in the morning
So many things to do today
Where should I start?
Maybe if I practice martial arts?
No, not that one first
Children, allow me to think!
Slam, pitter-patter, tee-hee!
Pssst, psst, what will she do?
Break open the blinds
I think I'll read a little while
Or maybe I should writer
"Mine! All mine! Gimme!"
Children, I've had enough!
She's had enough, she says.
Never mind! On second thought
I'll just go back to bed!

8-14-2021

This was written on a day I wanted to go back to bed but still light-hearted and a bit of satire.

"It matters not what people think of you when you are seeking to do what is right according to the Word of God. What matters most is that you live in such a way that when you get to heaven the Lord will say, 'Well done, good and faithful servant.'"

11-1-2015

****

Sleepy Eyes

Sleepy eyes and tired me
Did that nut fall from that tree?
I'm not sure what I did see
I'll lay me down and snore a z.

When I wake I'll crack that nut
See if I can tell you what
I will do to make it cut
That will be an accomplishment.

Never fear if that don't work
I'll cut a piece of your red shirt
I'll set it in the pot to perk
And when it's done I'll make a skirt

I'm sure I'll think of what to do
I'll pick up that old blackened shoe
Throw it at the tree and then you
Can beat me all but black and blue.

7-6-2017

This was a fun one after a long day of doing schoolwork. This poem popped into my head, and off I went with it. Sometimes the ones that just flow make the best funny poems!

"Not everyone is a child of God, but every true child of God will be protected by His steadfast love which does endure forever."

11-7-2015

****

It's Me Allergies

Blow me nose and rub me eyes
Don't you know? Don't you realize?
This whole things just a'killin' me
The pollen from that big ole tree
It's me allergies!

Me nose is runnin' from me face
It keeps increasin' it's own pace
Don't you realize? Don't you see?
The problem from that honey bee?
It's me allergies!

It's comin', I feel it! Atchoo!
In fact, I'll e'en give you a clue
Me eyes waterin' and itchees!
Me nose clogged up, it's a...a...sneeze!
It's me allergies!

This congestion I have to say
Please, I beg you, take it away!
Don't forget I need honey tea
Me chest sends forth apology
It's me allergies!

The kleenex, I must wipe me nose!
Hey wait! It's fallin' there it goes!
I wipe it up and then I see
It goes again… Away with thee!
It's me allergies!

Again, again, it happens so
Is it comin' from me big toe?
Just you wait if you don't believe
I'm hopin' to have a reprieve.

It's me allergies!

The fever has come once again
I cough so much I've lost me brain
I'll have revenge on that ole tree,
The flower, and grass, and bumblebee!
It's me allergies!

I sneeze again, atchoo! Atchoo!
I think me face is turnin' blue!
I'm tellin' you, I have no glee
I'm done I say….atchee! Aaaaaa-tchee!
It's me allergies!

Sniffle, snuffle, bring the tissues
When can I please lay down and snooze?
Me allergies are killin' me
Naught else but that can this thing be!
It's me allergies!

No, those tears are startin' to run
Scratchy eyes! Yeah, this should be fun!
I'm goin' on an itchin' spree
No worries, though, I'll rub happily!
It's me allergies!

It's time for me to take me pills
I'm startin' now to get the chills
Snort, hack, cough, yeah, let me be
I'll take me nap and you will see
It's me allergies!

I'll wake up and will start again
With this whole bus'ness now and then
I know that this is agony
And I will face it grumpily.

It’s me allergies!

Tell me, how long must I bear this?
Oh, when will I fin’ly have bliss?
I’m sure that we can all agree
No longer will I talk to thee,
‘Bout my allergies!

8-20-2022

I dedicated this poem to my oldest son after discussing allergies. He suggested I write a poem about them. Actually, it was a lot of fun, and he even suggested I write a few extra lines about pills and eyes. My son and grandson laughed over it and understand as they suffer from allergies.

****

Frizzy!

There was a time when I was dizzy
I checked my hair and it was frizzy
I asked, “How do I know
Whether I should forego
Doing my hair while I’m so busy?”

I didn’t want to have melodramas
So I gave my hair a lick and promise
I happened to see the clock
Realized suddenly in shock
It was time for me to put on my pajamas!

****

The Singer

The recruiter and all of his committee
Were sitting around being quite witty
They were wanting to see
Who could sing prettily
And it made me feel, oh, so giddy.

I decided to sing a little ditty
'Cause I felt my voice was so pretty
I howled out a note
That got stuck in my throat
And it sounded like it was all gritty!

11-4-2015

Both of these were written on the same day. My youngest daughter has frizzy hair like I had when I was a child so I thought I'd write it about her. The second one sounded like something that would happen to me. Besides, I like limericks!

****

Satire for the New Year!

Out goes the old and in comes the new
I really do think this isn't for you
The things I think that you try to do
Are old-fangled ideas and surely askew.

You are the embarrassment to us, the few.
(We are growing stronger daily) and who,
Want to tell everyone the real worldview
Stupidity is right now not what's true.

Because we know what is best for you
Turn it all over to us because you're the fool.
Don't argue, berate or try to see through
Anything that's contrary to my point of view.

I am the smartest there was of anyone's crew!
Look at what I've done, it's all very new
(Ok, don't look because I didn't really do
What I said) and I'm the best, better than you!

If you don't let me do what I want to do
I will call you a bigot, racist and a few
Other good names to make you think you
Are an idiot. However, I'm the king's fool!

12-22-2015

Chapter 3

Dealing with

Death…

Time and Grief

Haven't we heard that time
Heals all wounds? Do you mind
If I disagree? They remain
And we live with the pain

No, not in the same way
The mind has to defray
The pain sometime, somehow
Normal is not normal now!

The mind has to make a new
Normal to make it through
The next day and then soon
You have a new normal hewn

But even then the pain goes on
The sudden thought, the memory song
Brings deep sadness within our soul
No, only the Lord can make us whole

That is the only way to make
It work in our minds and take
Time to stray from pain and grief
The way eventually to find relief.

6-29-2017

My dad had just died days earlier. Someone sent me a saying that said once we lose someone, we don't return to normal. Even after all these years, something can strike me: a memory, a reminder, or even just a mood, and I end up in tears. Mostly there is relief from the grief but not always.

****

The Scream in the Night

I heard a scream in the night
And turned to look at those
Who were around me then
But they didn't look up in fright

They didn't seem to hear a thing
So I asked myself why they
Didn't move or respond
Is this a mirage or a dream?

I realized then that it was just I.
The silent scream came from within
And stayed where none could hear
Oh, the ache of it made me cry.

Did you hear that in your heart?
Did you feel the echo through?
Were you screaming along with me?
Did it bring to you a sudden start?

Is this bellowing whisper affecting you?
My dad is dying, now, and then
He will be gone away from me
It's so hard to comprehend, too!

My heart sent forth that scream
And now I'm hurting in my soul!
I'm sorry if it's what startled you
I wish this were only a dream.

Yet I know the Lord is still in control
No matter what is happening
No matter how horrible things go
Despite the pain, He will make me whole!

This was written June 12, 2017, shortly before my dad passed away. We already knew it would happen, but knowing and suddenly realizing he would no longer be around are two different things. It was a rough time with many other things happening in the background.

****

"I wonder if this is what a broken heart feels like. Sometimes, when I think about Dad and other things going on in my life, a hurt seems to start from within my heart, go into my shoulders, and then my arms. It hurts so bad that I feel like someone just pounded me."

7-19-2017

****

It's Just That I'm Missing You!

It's not that I wanted you in pain
It's not that I needed to complain
It's not that I felt you should remain
It's just that I'm missing you!

It's really a hard time right now
It's really a sorrow on the brow
It's really hard to understand how!
It's just that I'm missing you!

Now, it's a hurting in the heart
Now, it's a stinging from the dart
Now, it's aching that won't depart!
It's just that I'm missing you!

One day the pain might go away
One day the pain might portray
One day the agony might give way!
It's just that I'm missing you!
Dear Dad, it's just that I'm missing you…

6-26-2017

I still miss hearing my dad's voice even though I can recall the sound of his voice at times. It's not the same as hearing him speak. In one sense, this is a tribute to all of those loved ones who have passed on before us. I hope and pray you think about your loved ones and keep their memories alive!

"Pray for those in need...not just the ones you love, but also the unlovely."

****

Father's Day

Father's Day, they come and go
Whether for Dad, husband, or son
The years they always ebb and flow,
And you lose them one by one.

Eventually, they'll seem to slow
And then there will be none!
Take my advice, and you'll bestow
Your love. Please, your help don't shun

One who raised you, helped you grow
This poem's only half begun.
Yet your father may not show
That his life is almost done

I feel this caution apropo
Because he soon may be gone
Hurry now! Tell him so!
Life's passing on and there's none

Who can keep their dad below
On this earth when their race is run!
We loved you, Dad, and we know
You knew it well whate'er did come
Goodbye, dear Dad, our love's aglow
And goes with you as your day is done!

6-24-2017

Each Father's Day is sad for me. How often did I forget his love for me? Oh, to have one more day to say how much I love him! If your dad is alive, don't wait! Go and let him know how much he means to you before it is too late.

"Don't be a people pleaser...be a pleaser of God and willing to obey Him in all things."

****

Hey World!

Hey world,
My dad just died
How dare you keep
Moving forward!
It's time to stop
And show regard
For a man who
Loved his fam'ly
We miss him so!

Hey world,
Don't just keep on
Rushing around
And leaving us
Broken and hurt.
I may just end
Up withdrawing
From you and quit
Until I heal!

Hey world,
I know you don't
Care any bit.
But I don't care
Either for you.
I'm tired and
I'm ready to
Ignore you so
There we all are.

6-17-2017

Life goes on even when a loved one dies. I hate this fact, but I thought my words could let the world know. It is quite humorous in one way, but in another, it's quite sad. In the end, I'm sure no one cared about my little tantrum, but it hurt seeing everyone enjoying life when my dad died.

****

Death of a Father!

I long to tell you my heart
But it seems
I really can't even start

How can I
Let you know from my part?

The pain is there no matter
What I do
My heart is 'bout to shatter
Do you hear
Me above the chatter?

I love you, dearest father
But I can't
Express it altogether
The same as
My sister and daughter

Does this mean I don't love you
Like they do?
Does this mean my soul's askew?
Why can't I
Express myself as they do?

No! A thousand times more...No!
My love for
You is just as strong; although
My words may
Not have quite the same flow!

My head is really aching
Tears, yes, they
Come and go...my heart...breaking
The sorrow,
Sadness and loss is taking

It's taking its toll on me
My dear dad,
Don't you understand and see?

I love you
I'm sure you will agree!

I love you so much it's pain
That you're gone
I'll miss you and there's this chain
About my
Chest that's 'bout to break in twain

Give me some time and I'm sure
That chain will
Ease and I'll learn to endure
The hurt in
My soul. I'll become pure.

Like the gold!
I love you, Dad!

6-15-2017

This was written for my sister. She does not enjoy writing. After our dad died, she sent me an email with her heart hurting because she couldn't express herself. It was short and a cry of pain, and this is the poem it became.

"Even in the most difficult times, praise God for His goodness towards you. All deserve hell but, if you are a true believer, He has given you life eternal."

****

What's Going to Happen When?

What's going to happen when
I go and stand by your chair
Look at the area you sat in
And see you aren't there?

What's going to happen when
I walk about the house
Remember the steps you took
What feeling will this espouse?

What's going to happen when
I turn 'round to speak your name
To say something I've thought of
Or go to you a hug to claim?

What's going to happen when
I want to chat with my dear dad
And remember there will be none
No more talk, and oh, will I be sad?

What going to happen then?
I know the tears will once again flow
There will never be a time on earth
Again that your voice I will know.

What's going to happen then, dear Dad?
What's going to happen then?

6-28-2017

Chapter 4

Familiar Tunes

With New Words

(Tune of Here Is Love Vast As the Ocean)

You endured that cross for my sin
And You made me clean and pure
You're the One who satisfies me
Your salvation, very sure!
You're the Lifter up of my head
My Refuge and Secret Place
You're the One Whose Name is holy
Author, Fin'sher of my faith!

As I meditate upon You
Seek to follow Your pure will
You're my Glory and Sustainer
You, my heart, alone can fill
You preserve me from all evil
The Retainer of my soul
You will take me through the trials
Be like You, the final goal!

You forgive all my transgressions
You are faithful! You are just!
There is none upon earth like You
You alone, worthy of trust!
You will never sleep nor slumber
You're the One Who shows favor
You are sweeter than the honey
You're my Shepherd and Maker!

10-9-2015

The Bible is so very rich with allegories, descriptiveness, and many other ways in which it shows how great God is. Because of this, I like to use descriptive words from it.

****

(Sung to the song of Let Me See This World, Dear Lord)

Let me see my sin, Dear Lord,
As though I were looking through Your eyes
My heart and the blackness within, Dear Lord,
The sin for which You died.
Let Your horror of sin be my heartbreak
Blur mine eyes with tears of agony.
For if once I could see my sin the way You see
I would seek to hate my sin for love of Thee!

Change my sin sick soul, Dear Lord,
So that I will become more like Christ
Make me pure and white within, Dear Lord,
Give me strength to follow You in this fight.
May I stand for truth whatever happens
Give my heart holy tenacity,
For Your death on the cross is what gave life to me
Now, I want my life wholly given to Thee!

1-14-2017

I worked on this song for years. The Lord finally gave me the words after years of learning and growing. I realize now that our souls must be completely given over to the Lord for us to change. Not only that, but for us to even want to change, the Holy Spirit must give us that desire. I hope this stirs up a desire in your heart to change and become more like the Lord Jesus Christ.

"As we draw nearer and nearer to the end of time, expect to be persecuted for your faith!"

****

(Tune of Pass Me Not,
O Gentle Savior)

1. Suff'ring is a part of You, Lord
Persecutions come
Since I'm Your adopted child
I should expect some.

Chorus:

Suff'ring, Suff'ring,
Was the Savior's part
If I'm following His teachings
I will feel that dart

2. Men don't want to hear about sin.
They're content to be
Just the way they are right now, friend,
They think they are free.

3. They will hate you as they hated
The Lord and Savior Christ
We're no better than our Lord is
His grace will suffice.

4. Rejoice for we're partakers
In Christ's sufferings
He suffered, bled, and died for us
This, our offering!

4-6-2017

The Bible talks about true believers suffering because they follow Christ. No matter what happens, we are no better than Jesus Christ when He came to earth, so we can't expect to get away without suffering or persecution. Regardless, God is worthy of all praise!

****

(Tune of Sweet Hour of Prayer)

Adversity and suffering
No time of sleep and slumbering
God promised us in His own Word
Be strong, His armor we must gird.
Affliction will be sure to come
So study now do not succumb
We must begin His Word to learn
Prepare to stand and be forewarned

No longer time to play the fool
Satan thinks that this earth he rules
Let's stand and follow what is right
Knowing ill-treatment is in sight.
"Take up your cross and follow Me,"
Jesus commands for that's the key.
The fight is long and hard this way
The Lord His help He won't delay.

It's coming soon, it's coming soon
Pick up your cross night, morn, and noon.
Remember that the fight is on
It's easy now but not for long.
For speedily we'll face the pain
Then will we stand or turn away
From our dear Savior and His Word
Or do what's right despite our fear?

June 2021

This song was written after following the news of the persecuted pastors in Canada in 2021 during the so-called Covid-19 pandemic. During this time, pastors were told they could not preach and churches were shut down. We should be aware of what is going on with our brothers and sisters around the world.

Chapter 5

Persecution

The Time

The time is now
The time is here
The time is close
And, oh, so near.

It does begin
To look like we
Are almost done
This is my plea.

Today's the day
Of salvation
Don't wait too late...
Separation.

God's law still stands
His grace gave all
And now His time
Answer the call.

Tomorrow may
Be way too late.
There's one sole way
And that's the gate.

The gate's narrow
And fits alone
A single one
Please! Don't postpone!

Turn to Him now.
He waits for you
His arm ope wide
To let you through.

Forgiveness must
Be granted to
The one who is
Repentant true.

Then follow God
Obey His will
His grace is gi'en
Design fulfilled!

10-21-2015

****

I Thought About You…

I thought about you…
I didn't know your name
I really had no claim
Except you know the Lord
And seek to keep His Word.
I am your sister in Christ.
He is the One Who paid the price.

I thought about you…
I prayed for God's help
for you and I felt…
No, I knew He would
Since you greatly withstood
And suffered such pain and loss.
You took a stand for the cross.

I thought about you…
I'm praying you will have peace
And that it will not cease

No matter what comes your way
God will be your help and stay
During your hardest time
May the Lord be your paradigm.

10-14-2015

****

Persecuted Believers

Paying the price for being a Christian
Expecting to suffer for Christ's sake
Resting in the Lord no matter what comes their way
Seeking Christ in the midst of hard times.
Earnestly contending for the faith no matter what happens.
Casting all their care upon the Lord.
Using persecution to show others Christ's love
Taking one day at a time.
Entering heaven triumphantly
Depending upon the Lord all the time.

Believing tribulation makes them more like the Savior.
Existing to obey God's will despite oppression.
Letting the Lord be their stay.
Instead of fighting back, they let the Lord do it His way.
Excited to follow God's will in the face of ill-treatment.
Viewing God as gracious in spite of expulsion from others.
Exacting death upon sin regardless of being told to sin upon pain of death.
Remembering the Lord and His Word without regard to affliction.
Spending time in prayer for unbelievers and unlovely that hurt them.

****

We Are Praying

We pray for you
Our brothers and sisters in Christ.
We are praying
As you give up yourself and leave this life.

We pray for you.
We see you fall one by one
We are praying
That the Lord's will be done.

We pray for you
Asking Him to give you strength and grace
We are praying
Knowing that one day it's what we will face

We pray for you
Our hearts in a jumble of agony and pain
We are praying
Watching the ground, knowing your blood will stain

We pray for you
As you stand true to His Word
We are praying
That your persecutors, the gospel will have heard.

We pray for you
And we know the gospel won't return void.
We are praying
One day the devil's power will be destroyed.

10-08-2015

****

Pray For the Persecuted Church!

The days have come and gone
For those who've done no wrong.
They've certainly had to be strong
Because of what they've undergone.
Pray for the persecuted church!

The only point that isn't liked
Is doing what, in God's eyes, is right
According to God's perfect light
For that they are truly disliked .
Pray for the persecuted church!

They're treated with utmost disdain
Those who hate God seek to complain
And Christians end in terrible pain
They are sometimes even slain.
Pray for the persecuted church!

We here in the West are complacent
From pleasures there needs estrangement
Praying is the perfect arrangement
It teaches us to be still and patient.
Pray for the persecuted church!

The hurting ones need courage and strength
To stand tall, they need all the prayers
Their pain should be our hurt and tears
And distress for them in our hearts at length.
Pray for the persecuted church!

Scripture is clear, Remember those
That are in bonds, and also their foes

God might possibly be fully disposed
With His love around them enclose.
Pray for the Persecuted Church!

You see the church only makes a mark
When she follows God to finally embark
Upon His mission not hers then the spark
Of sacrifice will be her watermark.
Pray for the persecuted church!

Only then will the world get to see
The church, though in pain, she is free.
She chooses to follow Him not a prithee
Faith but obedience doing it coloss'ly.
Pray for the persecuted church!

She will give up her life for her Lord
And His will, her life be outpoured
Her own will is considered deplored
Then in heaven she'll receive her reward.
Pray for the persecuted church!

So our duty is quite clear to us now
We are bound only to God to bow
His Word we follow and avow
Persecution He truly will allow!
Pray for the persecuted church!

9-30-2015

"Because of our freedom in the West, ours is the greater responsibility to pray for our brothers and sisters who are being persecuted for their faith!"

****

It's Coming

It won't be long
Before it's here.
The day is coming
And it's near.

Are you ready?
Can't you see?
It's not just them
But you and me.

Believers now
Must ope their eyes
A serious look
And now realize…

We see it some
Not quite so clear
But others saw
It coming here.

They warned us then
They cried aloud,
"Do you not see
That darkened cloud?

"It's o'er the hill
A little ways
It won't be long
Wake from this daze!
"It's time to wake
It's time to stand
It's time to share
God's Word so grand!"

We listened not
When then we heard.
We thought it was
To be ignored.

We laughed away
The point and said,
"Ha! We have time!
Not much to dread!

"We will do it.
It will be great.
You are too serious
Stop! Don't debate!

"Give the people
What they want.
A play, music…
Don't be blunt."

Time is wasting
Please don't delay.
The sky, once bright,
Looks bleak and gray.

The time is close
And soon will be
A thing that's past
For you and me.

You see, this thing
We caution you
Is our freedom
In sharing truth.

Once that's gone
You will soon see
No time to share
But time to flee

Or take a stand
Face the fallout
And then realize
This is about…
PERSECUTION!

7-6-2015

I wrote this thinking the time was near for persecution. It certainly seemed so at that time. However, the years show it's nearer now then when I originally wrote it.

****

Too Close

We said before
We'll say again
The sky's not grey
It's black, my friend.

The looting and
The rioting, too.
The laws have changed
I'm sure you knew.

Our freedoms once
We held so dear
No longer ours
But gone, I fear.

The shocking wave
The tsunami
Has piled above
And now are we…

About to fall
Were it not for
Our dear Savior
And risen Lord.

So trust in Him
Without delay
Read His sweet Word
Fail not to pray.

Stand up for God
And do what's right
First death then your
Soul will take flight.

8-11-2022

We still haven't lost all our freedoms, but the sky is now black with rolling clouds piling up on top of each other. If you haven't come to the Lord, do so without delay!

Chapter 6

Sister

Poems

A Sister Is…

A sister is…
A friend who is there to hear you out
To discuss what happens to you
To encourage you, without a doubt,
And to cheer you when you are blue
Waiting to make it through that last bout.

A sister is…
A friend who will help in time of need
Whether it be with suggestions
Of how to solve the problem in deed
Or support with the emotions
If that is what is decreed.

A sister is…
A friend who will joke and have fun
Laugh at the crazy things said by you
And definitely not to be outdone
She reminds you of the hullabaloo
In early years by both of you, begun.

A sister is…
A friend who's there through thick and through thin
Someone who waits on arguments to cease
Who will patiently forgive the sin
Of the other and hope to increase
The level of friendship within.

So you see, it's very true
Sisters can be much more than just friends
A promise, a hope, and a new
Desire that can make them transcend
A previous relationship, a view
Of what a sister can be in the end.

6-10-2017
Dedicated to my sister

****

Sister Lovely

Sister lovely, sister true
What I wouldn't do for you
It's time for us to have fun, too
And then share a sis review
What that is, I have no clue

Sister lovely, sister mine
Shall we set out to design
A house that really is sublime
Then the chairs we will recline
And rest awhile, for a time.

Sister lovely, sister dear
I want to bring to you some cheer
Don't think I am not sincere
Maybe we should both appear
Tell our story, be austere!

So instead, let's laugh awhile
Tell each other jokes and smile
Pretend we are the queens in style
Be the judge and hold a trial
Then we'll do our laundry pile!

6-21-2017

Even after my dad died, I did have some silly times. Yes, this was one of them.

"Is Christ the One Who fills your heart with joy and commitment? Examine and prove yourself...make sure you are a true child of God!"

9-14-2015

Chapter 7

Grandson

Poems

Dearest Anthony, our grandson,

Both Avo and I want you to know
We send
Big hugs
And kisses
Our love
Your way

Whether you go to the moon
Or stay
Fly around
Ride horses
Finish school
Sing songs

Even if things don't go your way
Please know
We always
Love you
Whatever happens
Forever eternally!

From Bonbon
(Violet Inez)
8-25-2021

This was done for my grandson. He was feeling low at the time and I wanted to encourage him.

"When it seems like you are wasting your life by serving the Lord, just remember that it is at that time that you are truly gaining your life. You are not defined by the world if you are a true believer...you are defined by Christ."

9-14-2015

****

Reading Time!

When it's time for books
I'm sure you'll agree
We must read together
Both Anthony and me

For books are important
It's the blue decree
Or was it the green one?
Wait! That's for the tea!

Regardless, no matter,
We've decided, you see
That we must read books
Despite the beatle-bee!

It fuzzes and buzzes
And yells, "Verily!"
As we go to sit down
In our book-reading tree.

We yell out to each other,
"The secret, our key
Return, return and go
You must leave us be!"

Normally, it works
Then we can be free
To read our great books
With our yummy iced tea!

We'll read the red ones
And blue ones

The hat ones
And shoe ones
Finish up with the bread ones!

Next, for the great puns
And sad puns
The new puns
And glad puns
Finally, the eight puns!
And then we're done
With the ones
And the puns.

We'll close up our book
Send hugs and kisses
Give a smile to boot
And short reminisces.

And then we'll
Say goodbye!
Only for now
Of course.
Love you!

8-7-2021

This was a fun one for my grandson! He loved Dr. Seuss books at the time, so I wrote him a couple of poems in that style.

"As we spend time with the Lord in prayer, if we are truly focusing on Him, our hearts will quieten down just as a babe quietens down when the mom speaks calming words of love. We will realize that He is in control and nothing happens without His permission."

9-21-2015

Chapter 8

Husband

Poems

My Husband

What a kind and thoughtful man you are
So considerate of those you love
Willing to take the brunt of things
For your family thereof

You consider the other person
And seek to do what's right
No matter how they treat you
You help make their load light

I see the depth of help you show
Not just the ones whom you deem close
But equally helping 'gardless of spite
And kindness from your heart flows

You share the truth in kindness and
Refuse to spread forth lies
For, as you know, it's the only way
To give yourself 'thout compromise.

You love your family and seek to help
Them become the best they can
Then when they've grown you want
Them to do right, take their own stand.

But even better, I want you to know
I love you so much simply because
You are my husband and you do right
And no matter that we have as flaws

You love me despite what I have done
Regardless of what happened to us
You heart continues to beat out your love
And that is the way it is thus.

So saying that, I'm sharing with you
This poem about you from my heart
I love you more today than I did
Many years ago, we met at the start.

You're the best husband there ever was
And I'm thankful to the Lord for you
In a heartbeat I'd marry you over again
Because I know your love for me is true!

6-12-2017

We went through some rough times when my dad died. This was written for my husband to let him know that I loved him even with all that was happening!

"Do you think it may be possible to get to heaven following your own path instead of God's? It's better to be prepared and find out what God has to say from His Word. Don't take that chance that you will find yourself in the lake of fire."

09-01-2015

****

I Thought

I thought I knew what love was
When we first met
Many, many years ago
But I regret
To tell you what is so
I didn't know.

I thought I knew what love was
When we began courting
It was an exciting time
While we were comporting
Together in our prime
Each occasion...sublime.

I thought I knew what love was
When our vows were complete
We looked each other in the eyes
Knowing they were concrete
With no disguise
Our marriage...the prize!

I thought I knew what love was
When our first came along.
We were so excited
Ready to stand strong
And raise him...delighted
But trying to be longsighted.

I thought I knew what love was
When our children grew.
To teach them all about the Lord
How they should make it through.
The future now unexplored
And eternity's reward.

I thought I knew what love was
When some of our children left
The nest to take flight
Even feeling bereft.
God gave to me, despite
All, my husband who's my delight.

I thought I knew but didn't
I learned what true love was
From a man who sought to be
The likeness of Christ because
He knows this is best for him and me
For he desires to be godly.

I thought I knew but didn't
Watching my husband gave me
An understanding of true love
Which isn't gotten from worldly
Impact but from above.
May you always be
That witness of true love!

I love you, Sweetheart!

12-17-2015
For our anniversary

"Sometimes all we see is the hurt and brokenness in our own lives but others see the Lord in us because of that brokenness!"

8-26-2015

Chapter 9

Miscellaneous Poems Through the Years

Thanks, A Small But Powerful Word

"Thanks"
A word
Small but necessary
So important to use
Even when it seems useless
For tiny deeds done for us
At times, when it appears pointless, unnecessary
How do you feel when you are ignored
After helping someone even with the little things?
Why not treat others kindly and thoughtfully?
So take time to say it
Spread courtesy to those around
Who helped you today
Or even yesterday
Tell them,
Thanks!

11-8-2019

This was written for a publication called *Koinonia*. Let's be grateful for things that people do for us.

****

Mid-Term Exam

Before the test

I studied hard
What did I get?
I think I passed
You made me sweat!

I know the stuff
I know it well
But when it comes
I shall not fail!

When grading comes
I'll give a note
"Give me an A
To pass this boat!"

After the test...

I made an A
I passed the test
I studied hard
And did my best

Well, thank-you, sir
And thank-you, ma'am
I passed this hard
Mid-term exam.

I saw your face
A sight to see
And that's the truth
From A to Z

Fall 1986

This was my first ever attempt at writing a poem. I wrote it for my dad before I took the mid-term exam and then right after I finished. My dad thought it was funny, and I can remember him laughing when I returned home and showed it to him. I have no idea which course it was, but I passed!

****

The Wonder of Creation

So many things to catch our eyes
Help us to see, or make us surmise
Wonder gives us its own special prize
What holds us back from all of this?
Certainly, let us not be remiss
Wonder comes in its own disguise
At times we don't even recognize
What is right in front of our eyes!

Think of the flowers and birds and trees
So many colors and varieties
Styles and types of many degrees
Let me open my eyes, look all around
Beauty and awe...yes, I must expound
Animals and waterfall, insects and bees
So many creatures besides all of these
I love seeing flowers, and birds, and trees!

This wide open space my heart it did steal
That Wyoming wind that I so love to feel
Against my face, for me, that's my appeal
When I think on these things it brings to mind
The One who created and made this design
The awe and wonder in my heart does reveal
The thankfulness toward God I know is real
The wonder of nature I cannot conceal!

10-2-2019

I wrote this for my Humanities college class. We had to write on the wonder of something amazing and Wyoming is amazing to me! This is still one of my favorite poems.

"Fear is like a termite that eats away at the inner workings of the foundation. If you dwell on it, it will seek to destroy the peace that passes all understanding."

8-18-2015

****

Candle of Life

Life…
Tell me
What is life?
Can you describe it?
Or explain what it's about?
Or hold it in your hands?
Can you create it by speaking words?
Or snuff it out the exact same way?
Is it like a candle you can blow out?
Tell me, friends and foe alike, what exactly is life?
Do you struggle to understand the nuances of your life?
Can you construct a life by snapping your fingers?
So, I ask again, What is life?
What makes the substance of a being?
Life doesn't come from just anything
It always comes from God
Who alone gives life
To all beings
He is
Life!

5-9-2019

****

Cares

Do the cares bow you down?
Make you worry, make you frown?
Make your life turn upside down?
Make you forget there'll be a crown?

9-7-2016

****

Beauty

Beauty
Is not
Simply facial features
As people might think
It has nothing to do
With what is on the outside
More importantly, it has everything to do
With what is in the heart and soul
That shows through the eyes, the expressions, the attitude
The inner person looking out through the doors of life
Is your heart and soul, the real one that's you
Striving to have an attitude pleasing to the Lord?
Seeking to make His Word applicable to you?
Everyone fails but getting it's getting up
And striving to do what's right
In the eyes of God
Living life His way
God gives this
Person true
Beauty.

9-16-2022

****

Rain Fall

I watched the rain fall
It made me think of all
The tears I've cried
And the times I've sighed
The sin is so prevalent
And always evident
Of my fallen nature
That I want legislature
To make me do right.
I know I have to fight
But only the Lord can
Change my inner man.

I watched the rain fall
It made me feel so small.
I thought of that hour
When things went sour
Truth be told
You were already cold
You finally made it clear
When you pushed the spear
Through the heart
Then decided to depart
And really spread your lies
To make others despise…

I watched the rain fall
I thought I heard the call,
"Come follow Me, friend.
I will heal not rend
The brokenness of your soul
I will make you whole.

Whether sin from self or another
You will recover
Because I will heal you
Completely through.
Be My disciple and obey."
God calls...do it His way.

12-2-2015

Chapter 10

Relationship

Poems

Shattered Pieces and Broken Hearts

When I was young and the world ahead
I plowed through with my way instead
Of looking at those who were in my life
I chose to live in bitterness and strife

Looking back, I can see to my chagrin
What pain and loneliness it left me in
The sharp, hateful words said angrily
Leaving others hurting, in pain, and needy.

As I grew older and have seen the pain
We each have issues and should refrain
From hurting others in the soul through
Shattering pieces and breaking hearts, too!

Now, don't get me wrong in this matter
God's Word is truth and that does shatter
Through our sin and worthless iniquities
So truth spoken in love are surely the keys

But relationships are so fragile, easily broken
Even when, in the right way, it's spoken
Searching our hearts to shake out the pride
Of being right or thinking we're better, inside

The struggle of it all, what I see at my age
We can be so right yet not on the same page
As the other person who misunderstands
And then there are once again those bands

Holding tightly to keep us from fellowship
A whisper here, a lie there, just a little slip
"They aren't what you thought they were e'en
Though you always thought they've been a friend.

Did you think they were really like that?
No, you've been blinded, as a matter of fact."
So the relationships fail and then are gone
Such needless waste and really so wrong.

What happens if that person is swept away
From these shadow lands, no longer of clay?
What would we have left of that person then?
Regrets and no way the relationship to mend?

We are broken creatures, easily led astray
And seem to be under an influence, a sway
Hurtful words and shattered pieces scattered
Like the blood of our precious Savior splattered

The cross of Calv'ry, paid for our wickedness
So let's take the time to put away pride unless
You thank that more important than obedience
To the One Who died, you sit on the fence.

Yet, why break the hearts of loved ones?
Instead, break the sin, watch our tongues
According to His Word. We need truth in love
And unity that only comes from above.

Unity that says God is right and the truth.
We know that His Word will give all the proof
Needed, until then we trust Him wholly
And from sin and wickedness we should flee.

So, let's take time, mend our ways, you see
With each other e'en though we don't agree
We follow God's truth, how He wants it done
Since, from this earth, one day we'll be gone.

5-30-2017

Life is never easy with relationships. When we say things to each other, let's be mindful of how we say things. We may not always agree on minor things, but unity in God's Word is extremely important.

The whisperer may make you think your loved one is not who you thought they were, but, in the end, look at the loved one's character and the whisperer.

Find out who really has the issue. Read God's Word and see what He says about a whisperer in Proverbs. In the end, don't make your decision on emotion but on Scripture!

****

When the Heart Breaks

When it seems in your life
Things are going good,
You try to love and give
To those who don't want
To be loved by you…
Then the heart breaks.

When you seek to reach out
To one you've prayed for,
Did everything in your power
To show grace even when
The return was hard and cold…
Then the heart breaks.

When the dear one
Disappears from your life
Not because of their fault

And you wonder if
You will ever see them again…
As the heart breaks.

When your loved one
Is in so much pain you see
The brokenness and agony
In their life, the hurt brought on
By one who does not care…
And the heart breaks.

When the heart is broken
And the pain is too much to bear
The Lord whispers in your ear,
"Wait on Me, and I will give you strength,
It's hard, but wait...wait…
While your heart breaks.

"Now is the time of trials,
You still have much to learn,
I must prune you in the midst
Of the days on earth so that
You will me made into My image…
As your heart breaks."

The Lord is near and dear
Despite the hurt, the agony,
The pain within the heart.
We know the Lord is always
With us no matter what…
When the heart breaks.

6-15-2014

Psalm 119:67; Before I was afflicted I went astray: but now have I kept thy word.

Isaiah 40:31; But they that wait upon the Lord shall renew their strength; they shall mount up with wings as eagles; they shall run and not be weary; and they shall walk and not faint.

Hebrews 13:5; Let your conversation be without covetousness; and be content with such things as ye have: for he hath said, I will never leave thee, nor forsake thee. Lamentations 3:25-26; The Lord is good unto them that wait for him, to the soul that seeketh him. It is good that a man should both home and quietly wait for the salvation of the Lord.

"Relationships are never easy as we have to work at them. However, when one person works at it, and the other person does not, it's even more difficult to work through the problems.

Always remember that we are all sinners and need to take responsibility for our own sins."

****

Truth and Lies

I wish I could reach out…
And know I could trust you.
It's too soon, you see
A real change? Is it true?

I've tried to give you
The benefit of the doubt
To see beyond the lies
To give you an out…

Yet, it seems each time
It returns still the same
The truth and lie won't mix
So...who is to blame?

It makes no sense to me
I read the lies and wonder
What is true or a lie from you?
Relationships parted asunder…

Your talk is so very clear
I feel mine agrees...the same
But what you have done is…
Opposite to what you claim.

Your walk is also so very clear
So different from what you say
How I long for both to match
One true hope...just a ray?

I feel it slipping away
You say you're being true.
I know that isn't the truth
Because of what you do…

Don't let it slip away this time
You may never get them back.
Broken relationships...hard to restore
You will find you're off track.

When you lie about someone
The Bible is so very true.
You are a sword or sharp arrow
You hate that person, too!

It really then stands to reason
Apparently, you don't seem to care
To tell the truth about the one
You lied about...but would you dare

Make a clean breast of it all?
Put the lies away...please do!
Tell the truth...then you will see
The one who was wanted...YOU!

1-8-2015

This is definitely a hard one in my life as we lost not only one relationship but several that were pretty important to us.

To this day, those relationships still have not been restored. However, God can make all things right in His timing according to His will.

****

Family!

Family:
Husband and
Wife, maybe children.
Are grandchildren and greats
Involved, too? Whoever is along
Whether step-mom, step-grandparents, possibly other steps.
When they help each other, show love
Speak truth and do what is right according
To God's Word not what we decide in life.

Remember that God sacrificing His Son and us accepting Him
Into our lives, this makes us spiritual family in Christ.
Our responsibility? Seek to share the gospel with our
Physical family so they will be in heaven
With us for all eternity. The spiritual
Family is far more important than
Our physical family. How so?
Because of eternity in
Heaven or hell.
This is
Family!

8-24-2022

I wrote this because of my grandson and I dedicate it to him. He asked if I could do a poem on family, but he didn't want me to overdo myself.

What he didn't realize is that if I can't figure out a poem, I'll simply set it to the side. If it works, it works. If it doesn't, then I never write anything else on it.

He also thought that poems had to rhyme. When I told him they didn't, he was amazed. So I wrote this up without a rhyme. Anyway, he loved the poem. Since this section is about relationships, I though the poem on Family should be in here. After all, what better way to finish up relationships than to do an upbeat one about family?

Chapter 11

Abortion

Poems

Death to the Baby!

They live in the womb for nine months, dancing,
For a certain time, people call them a fetus
But they aren't a blob of tissue, they are alive,
As living as an ocean roar.
Is that to be considered life or death?
They are not a blob of tissue but babies.

Beautiful and precious are these unwanted babies
Who spend every moment growing and dancing
Not meant to be dismembered and thrown away to death.
Having lived their short life as a fetus.
Will they ever hear the ocean roar?
Will they ever know what it's like to be alive?

What is it like for you to be alive?
Why aren't they allowed, these precious babies,
To be able to experience hearing the ocean roar?
Will they know what it's like dancing
To the tune of life instead of as a fetus
Who will only exist for a twinkling then death?

Not to have someone's arms wrapped round them in death
As those who are allowed to come out alive.
This is what those must endure who are called a fetus.
Oh, the silent screams of those not allowed to be babies.
Not allowed to be part of the dancing
Of life and the sound of the ocean roar.

How charming and delightful is the ocean roar
So different from the implacability of death
Why can't we just let them continue dancing
With the joy and iridescence of being alive?
These poor souls who should have been called babies
But are ever and anon only labelled...fetus.

The horror of it, just imagine if YOU were a fetus.
It should be alluring but now is frightening...that ocean roar
That their voices should be drowned out as babies.
The pulling and tearing and smashing monstrosity of black death.
Never more to feel but terror and agony before the end...not alive
Always an emptiness in the womb and arms that should be dancing.

Can we sentence the fetus to a grisly and shameful death
While the ocean roars and we are still delightfully and divinely alive?
The scorned and hated babies are torn apart and not allowed to be dancing!

7-27-2015

This was painfully difficult to write which was during the time the videos surfaced about what Planned Parenthood was doing with baby parts. I do not understand how people can claim babies are only blobs of tissue and murder them. In the end, God is in control and will work all according to His will.

****

Why?

A baby in the womb is like a beautiful
bloom, not yet a full rose
gently, gently
Lovely in the grace of vacuum and water that flows
The babe ripples smoothly back and forth like the gentle

sea that rocks the ship,
moving, moving
'Til one day the tiny one will lose, on life the grip.
Why?

A baby in the womb is like a soft breath
of air needing the loving,
helping, helping
Tender care not the hard, angry fist of tearing
To show that rebels disrupt in opposition to the kind,
care of the holy One, God
screaming, screaming
They do not care but wear an obscure facade.
Why?

Animals are good, necessary in our life and even
can be considered an anchor
not knowing, not knowing
But without a soul, after God, they cannot hanker.
Many believe that only animals not children who die
are worthy for them to mourn,
wailing, wailing.
The little ones...ahhh, who cares if they are torn?
Why?

Why? I must ask myself as I ponder this horrible and
despicable
question that should not be but is true
lying, lying
Why are animals chosen over babies? Tell me anew.
Why not allow the gravity of the situation to be spoken of
again and so many times?
Sleeping, sleeping
Is it because there are some who don't want known...their
crimes?
Why?

Why is the uproar over a lion so much more important to
society than the little one in the womb?
Driving, driving
Why must that become their own miniature tomb?
The place that should be the protection of the wee one's
life until they can manage on their own?
Dying, dying
Whispering into nothingness the scream and the moan?
Why?

May God forgive us and make us the ones with a voice
for those who have no voice
speaking, speaking
Give us the same love that He has. Father to the fatherless.
Open your mouth and speak forth righteousness and plead
the cause of the poor and needy
living, living
They need someone to stand up for them against the
greedy.
Why?
Our duty! Our duty!

8-21-2015

I wrote this after the concern about a lion that had been killed and yet people could care less about the videos being posted on Planned Parenthood.

These are the days where evil is good and good is evil. We need to speak the truth of God's Word and not listen to the world's lies.

****

The Chilling Truth

Rose colored glasses
Was what we wore when younger
Until we found out

So naive were we
To think all were aboveboard
Doing what was right.

Simple-mindedness
Instead, we found out the truth
Then winter arrived…

The silent screams and
Moans of the babies broke out
They were deafening.

We heard them roaring
No longer the quiet sound
Of such ignorance.

We knew there was death
To the poor babies and some
Stood against the bloodshed.

In the end it was
Revealed that this was even
More than just murder.

More than simply taking
The miniature one's vigor
The chilling truth is…

The wee legs and arms
Being torn apart in vogue.
Sold for lucre.

The poor little life
Being snuffed out for earnings
Darkness approaching!

8-4-2015

Chapter 12

All About Time

Time

I saw the time run quickly by
I rushed to catch it with a cry
It sped its pace
As in a race
Until I wondered if I should try

Faster it went until I failed
My skin was pink and then it paled
The heart attack
Which gave me flack
And then my spirit, yes, it bailed.

What is the moral of this rhyme?
Should all mankind make it a crime?
To slow the face
Of the fast pace
Article of what we call time?

5-6-2019

****

Wasting Time?

Time
I wonder
What it is
That makes us think
We have all the time
In the world to follow ourselves
To chase our own dreams of selfishness
How much time does God really give us?

Can we justify wasting our time following worldly pleasures?
If we can, will God give us the green light
By saying, "Well done, good and faithful servant, you chose well,"
After making it to heaven and standing before His gracious throne?
Or will He look at us and shake His head in sadness
While our hearts accuse us of wasting our time while on earth?
How much time will we have squandered doing nothing in life?
Are we rationalizing what we don't do for the Lord?
Hoping we will skate by doing little to nothing?
Even spending time with the Lord is better
Than ignoring Him and expecting the world
Given to us on a plate
So stop wasting your time
One day you will
Answer to God
For your
Time!

9-16-2022

Chapter 13

Monologues

and

Short Stories

Behind the Mask

Oh, hi! Did you come to visit me today? I'm not sure what we will talk about because I've put on my mask. You see, I don't want you to know too much about me. Why not? Well, if I tell you all the things that have happened or share my innermost secrets, you probably won't return. What? You think I should tell you anyway?

Well, I can't! No, it's not because I hate you. Okay, well, maybe I do. I mean, I don't appreciate you telling me that I sin. Of course, I don't sin. Since I do everything that I should, you have no right to accuse me. What makes you think I even want to hear it? What will happen if I listen to you? More than likely, I'll fall apart, and everyone will know about it.

Why won't I listen? Ummm, well, you see, I put my mask on and don't want to take it off. I don't want anyone to see who I truly am. What if I become too vulnerable when I do that? After all, you would probably walk away in disgust. Also, how would I feel if you told everyone everything you found out about me? And what about this one: Do you think I would recover if everyone came back and made fun of me simply because I told you a few of my problems?

Everything costs something, I tell you! Yeah, everything is going great right now. No, I don't need you. Stay away from me! You know what? At this point, I'm barely hanging on, and you make it worse by telling me that I sin. Never mind! I don't want your friendship! Tell someone else who will appreciate what you have to say. No, I don't want to hear it, and I will keep my mask on!

You did what?!? Hold on! Let me adjust my mask. It seems to have fallen off slightly for some reason. Wow! That changes it all.

Let me get this straight.

First, You came to this earth and died on the cross for my sin!

"For God so loved the world, that He gave His only begotten Son, that whosoever believeth in Him should not perish, but have everlasting life." (John 3:16)

Again, **WOW!!** Why? You, the God of heaven and earth, the Creator of the universe, You, the One Who takes care of all things and keeps it running. You came as a baby, grew up, lived a perfect life, suffered more things than I can imagine, and died on the cross. Why would You do that? And, for me? I know I sin, even though I try to hide it from people. Amazing that You would do that.

Second, they buried You, and You rose again the third day!

"For I delivered unto you first of all that which I also received, how that Christ died for our sins according to the scriptures; and that he was buried, and that he rose again the third day according to the scriptures..." (1 Corinthians 15:3-4)

I can't even begin to understand why You would do something so astounding for me. Because of my wickedness, I can't merit salvation no matter how hard I try, You say? Shall I tell You that I try so hard to do right, but I fail? Or did You know that already? The horror and decay within my heart reminds me daily that I can't do anything right. With that in my mind, why would I want to tell people about me? I'd rather have on the mask and pretend that nothing has happened. This could make a difference, though. I need to think it through.

Third, You bring me to Yourself and save me from my sins!

"Therefore as by the offence of one judgment came upon all me to condemnation; even so by the righteousness of one the free gift came upon all men unto justification of life. For as by one man's disobedience many were made sinners, so by the obedience of one shall many be made righteous. Moreover the law entered, that the offence might abound. But where sin abounded, grace did much more abound: that as sin hath reigned unto death, even so might grace reign through righteousness unto eternal life by Jesus Christ our Lord." (Romans 5:18-21)

I can actually be clean and righteous through the Lord Jesus Christ? He would give me eternal life? But, what about my mask? What about the fact that I lie steal, cheat, and do so many other things that I'm sure no one would want to know about me?

This amazes me! Why would You even want to save me as wicked as I am and have been for all my life?

Now, I want to take this mask off. Wait! Where did it go? Oh well! It no longer matters because I want the Lord Jesus Christ to rule my life. Will You forgive me for everything I've done wrong? Will You save me from my sins and take over my heart? Will You make me a new creation and give me a love for things that pertain to You instead of the world?

"Therefore if any man be in Christ, he is a new creature: old things are passed away; behold, all things are become new." (2 Corinthians 5:17).

****

Seeking the Answer to the Question

What is the question?

As I sat and pondered on the answer, my brain began to do some crazy things. First, it decided to wander into nothingness, so I had to bring it back under subjection. Second, it started thinking of other things that needed doing around the house. Third, when I tried to return to the question, it balked. Fourth, it then wandered back into nothingness.

Is this only me? Why can't I control my brain and do what I set out to do? Today isn't the only day it happened. It happens, well, um, hmmm, EVERY SINGLE DAY!

Don't get me wrong! Most of the time, I don't even notice it. After reading that last sentence, I now have to wonder where my brain goes. In fact, how do I ever accomplish anything?

It reminds me of those times that I know I have something specific I need to accomplish, so I get up to take care of it. On my way, I see two or three other things that need doing. By the time I arrive at my destination, I no longer know what I meant to do. I mill about for a few minutes then return to my starting place.

"Oh, yeah!" I tell myself. "Now I remember. Better get in there and do it immediately before you forget."

Promptly, I return and accomplish what I should have done an hour or so earlier.

Anyway, back to my original question. See what I mean? Subjection, brain! Subjection! Do NOT balk!

Returning to our conversation...I forgot. Where were we? Oh, that's right – the question. Oh, no! I forgot to write it down. Which question was I addressing?

The End

www.ingramcontent.com/pod-product-compliance
Lightning Source LLC
LaVergne TN
LVHW041124150826
845673LV00007B/2178

* 9 7 9 8 3 5 2 2 2 7 9 6 1 *